DRAW IT!

MONSTERS

100 spooky things to doodle and draw!

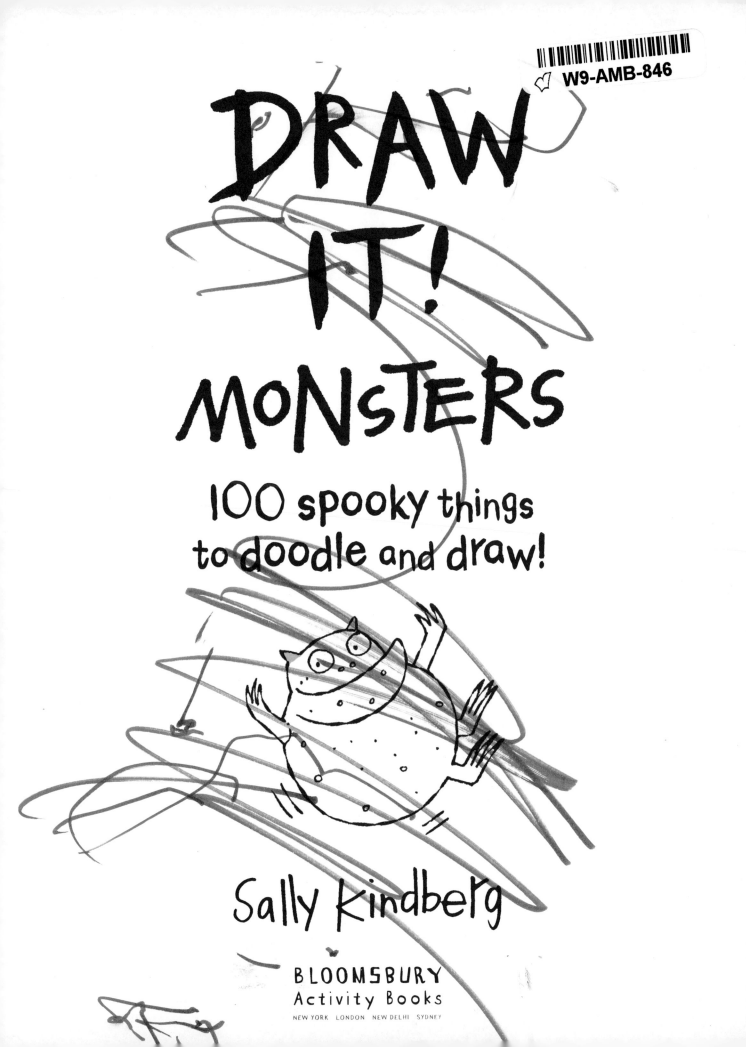

Sally Kindberg

BLOOMSBURY
Activity Books

NEW YORK   LONDON   NEW DELHI   SYDNEY

Draw a
superpowered
broomstick.

Draw the creatures that make these sounds.

Draw something horrible in this sewer.

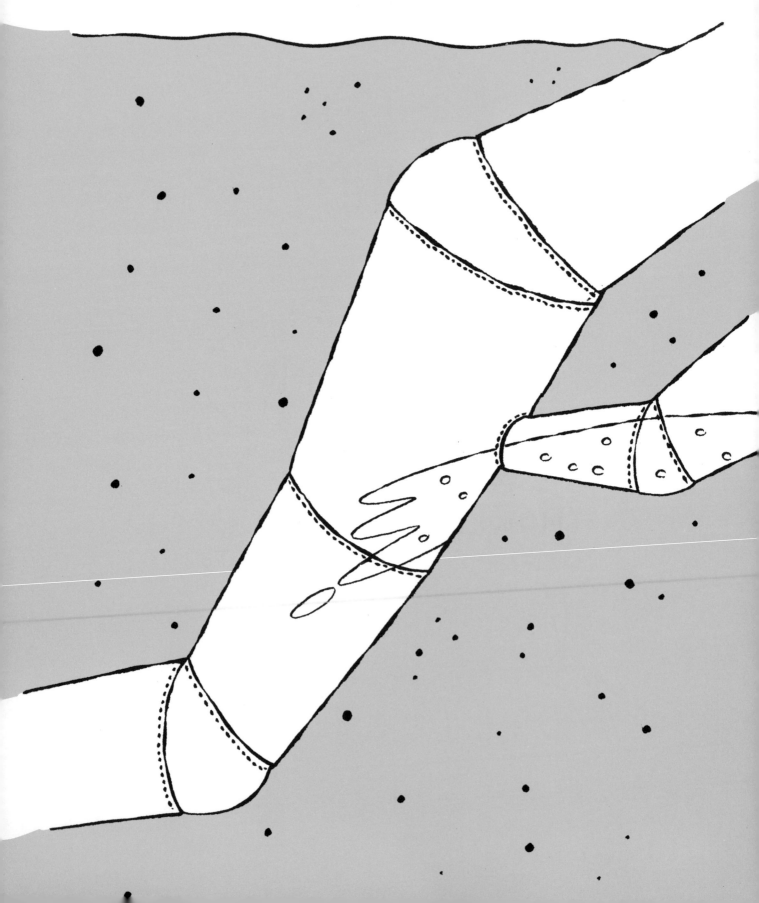

Draw some guests at the annual underwater monster party.

Draw the body for this creature.

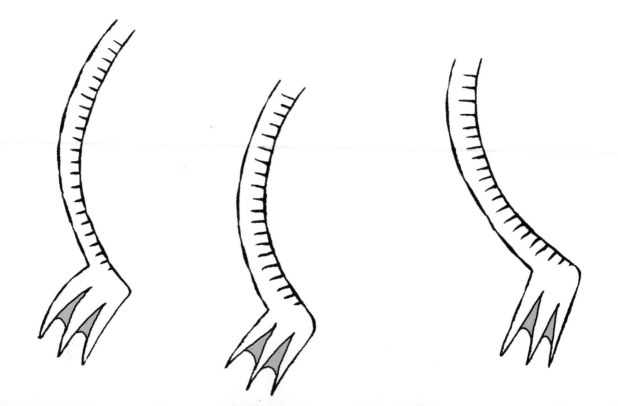

Draw some ghosts at the seaside.

Yum, yum . . . maggoty cookies! Draw some.

Oh dear.
You've been
abducted by
aliens. How did
that happen?
Draw it!

Draw a dragon family
having a picnic.

Draw a
ghoul
in love.

Draw some mummies waking up.

Draw someone
turning into
a werewolf.

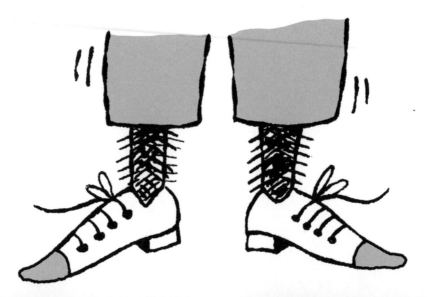

Draw some specs for these specters.

Draw a pet for
Dr. Frankenstein.

Draw some
hairy monsters.

Home smelling fresh and clean? Yuck! Draw some items to leave around for a lovely, sickening stench.

Draw a
monster
with a
terrible
cold.

Draw some false
teeth for a vampire.

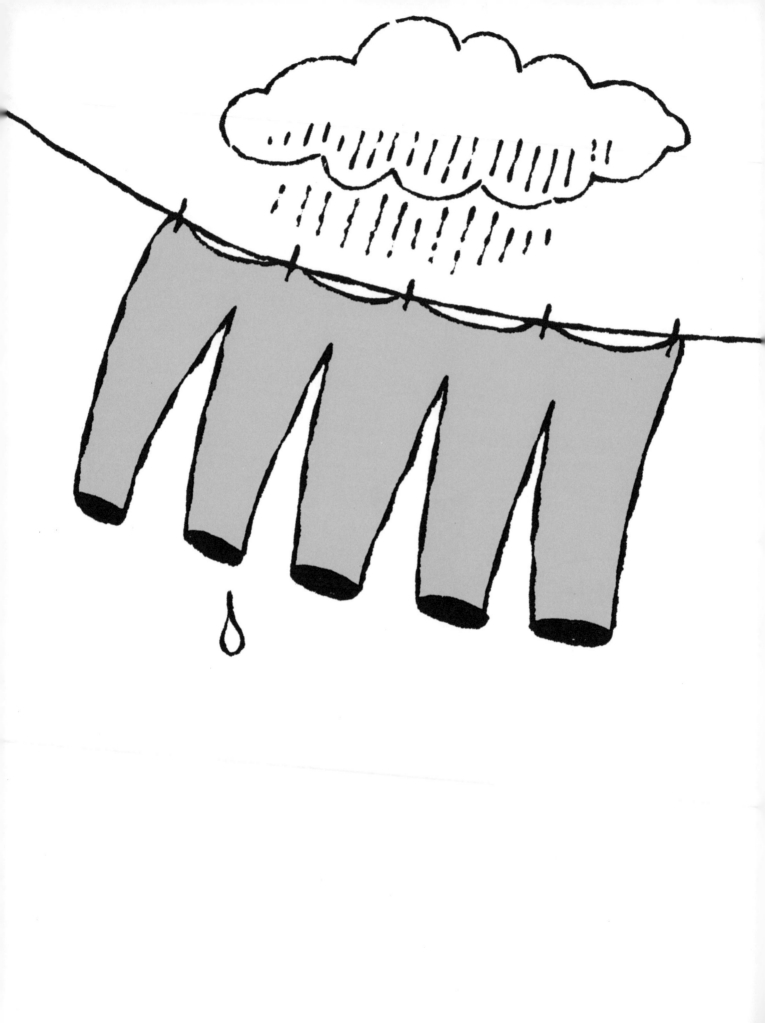

Draw a monster's
laundry hung out
to get moldy.

Draw 10 different creepy-crawlies.

Draw a zombie's
favorite snack.

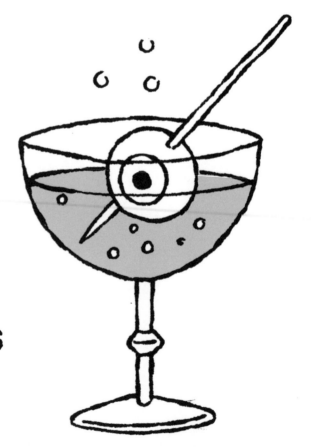

Draw a flying lesson.

Draw some monsters at their exercise class.

Draw a yeti
with killer
breath.

Draw a
monster's
nightmare.

Draw some
trolls doing
cartwheels.

Mmm . . . old sock-scented room spray. Draw a label for it.

Stinky

Draw a goblin in
a bad mood.

Draw a
baby ogre
out for
a walk
with his
mother.

Draw a giant
spider taking
her babies for
a stroll.

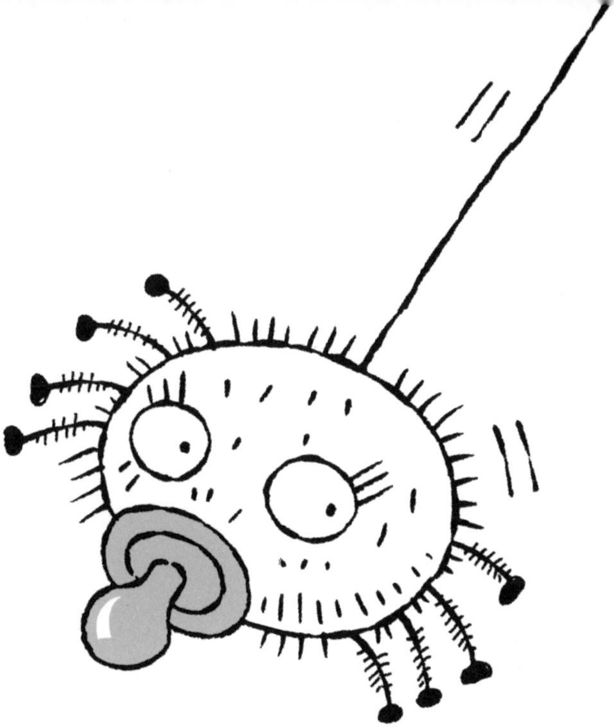

Draw something almost invisible.

Draw
a bone
cruncher.

Rattle
Rattle

Draw a puddle full of
bad-tempered toads.

Draw a
get unwell
card.

Draw some
monsters
having
a lurking
lesson.

SQUAWK!

Bushes
are good
for lurking
behind.

Whoops—these eyeballs have come loose. Draw their owners.

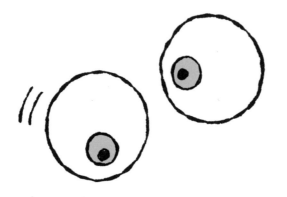

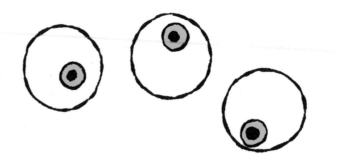

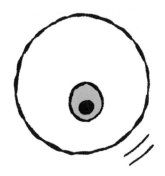

Draw a
monster's
ghastly grin.

Draw a
shy ghost.

Draw some hairstyles for these characters.

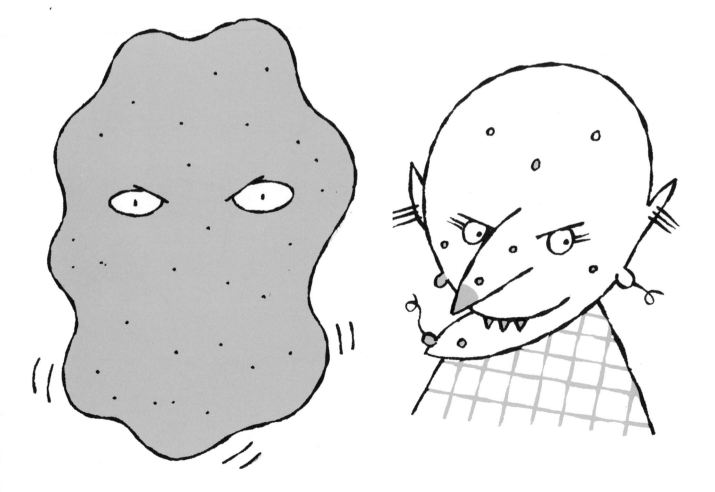

Draw
a ghoul
on a
bike.

Draw
some
gossiping
ghosts.

Draw some skeletons in this cupboard. How many can you fit inside?

Draw
something
that comes
out at
night.

Draw these monsters' family tree.

Draw a witch having a makeover.

Adds wrinkles in seconds!

Draw a map of Swampland™.

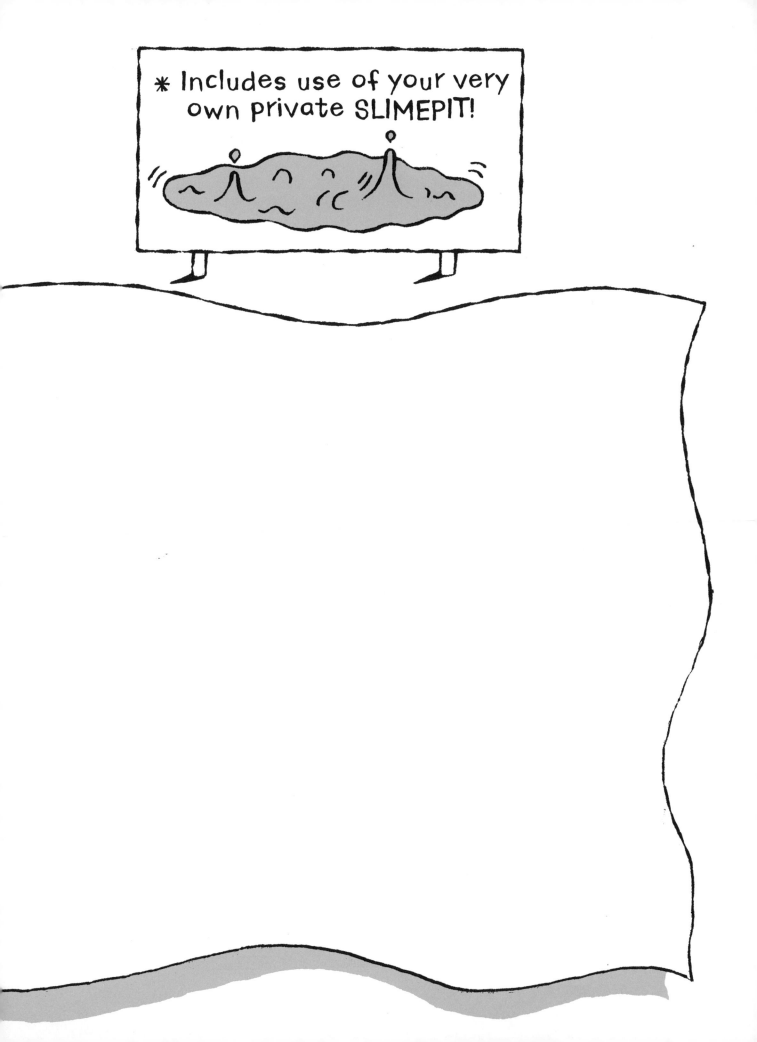

Draw a shape-shifter turning into something else.

Draw a witch on
a shopping spree.

Draw the Zombies' Sports Day.

Draw some ghastly styles for this claw boutique.

Draw a sea monster's favorite weather.

Draw a haunted suit of armor.

Draw a ghastly menu. Today's specials: Vomit Mousse and Pus Sausage.

Draw some boots designed to keep the damp in.

Draw a
cyclops with
a toothache.

Draw your escape from aliens.

Draw something
slithery that lives
under this stone.

Draw something unpleasant caught in this cobweb.

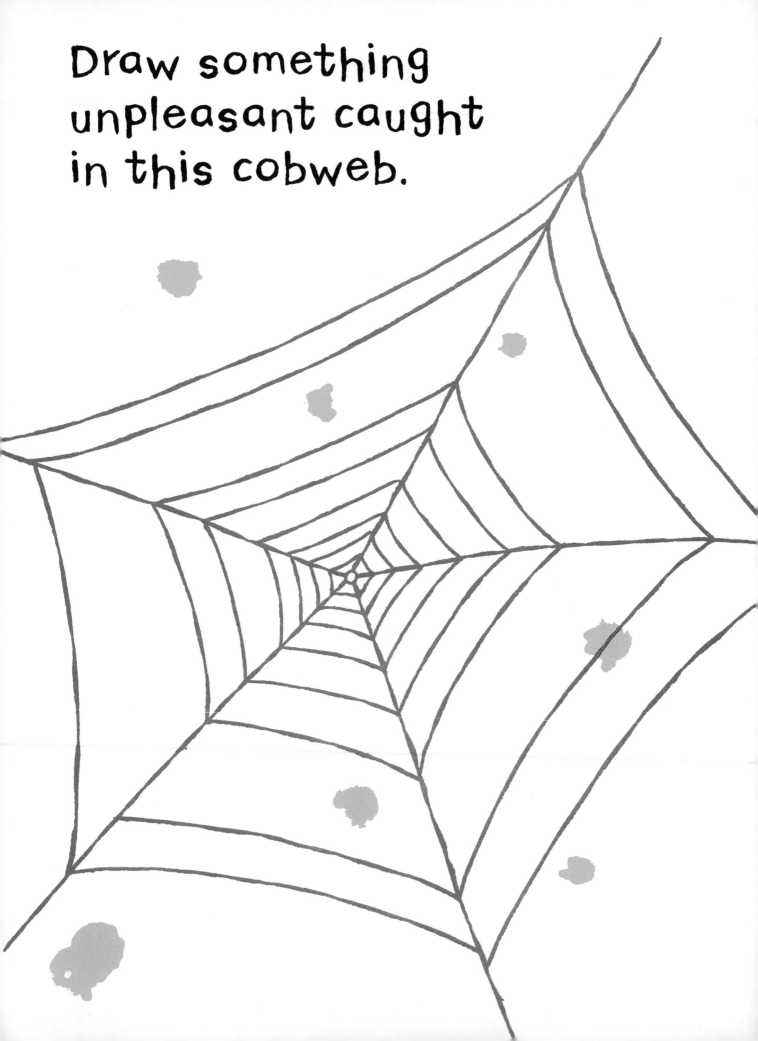

Draw some snakes in this pit.

Draw
what's in
a witch's
handbag.

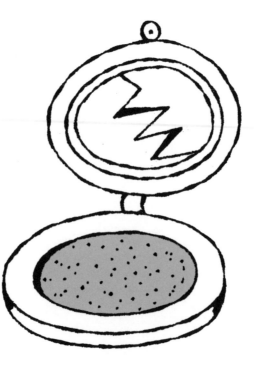

Draw some slimepaste.

Draw 3 finalists for this year's Ugly Contest.

Draw something
vile skulking in
this dungeon.

Draw a shriveled hand (useful for spells).

Draw 4 aliens on a shopping trip on Earth.

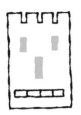

Draw a map of how to get to Creepy Castle.

You could use these symbols or make up your own.

Demon
Lair

Get Lost
Woods

Oh!

Sinking
Sands

Murky
Marsh

Draw some dance moves for the Monster Foot Bash.

Draw 3 things that make you shiver.

Draw an unwelcome mat.

Draw the front-page news for the *Daily Dreadful* newspaper.

Draw some oozing boils on this monster's face.

Draw some nasty potions on these shelves.

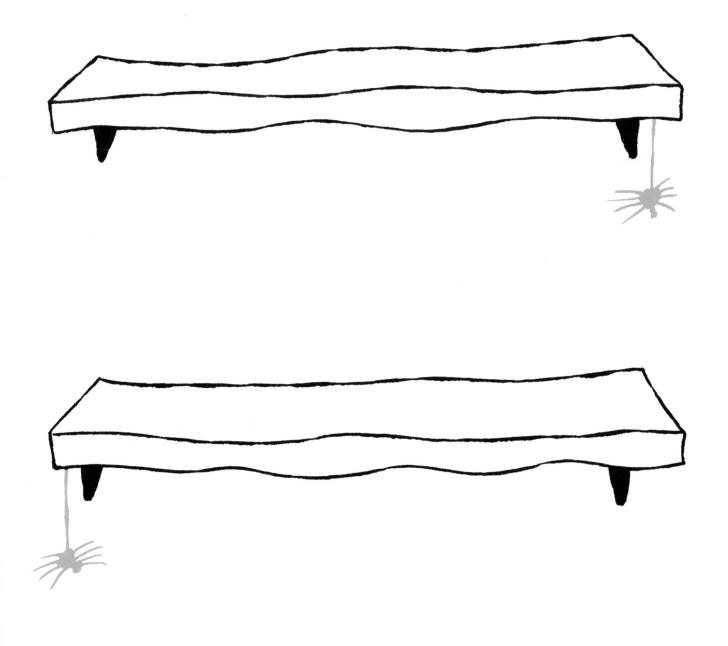

Draw the creatures that make these creepy shadows.

Draw tails for
these creatures.

Draw a giant
ship-munching
sea worm.

Draw some
ingredients for
a cauldron party.

Draw a clammy
handshake (or three).

Draw a night gurgler.

Draw how you might cross these sinking sands.

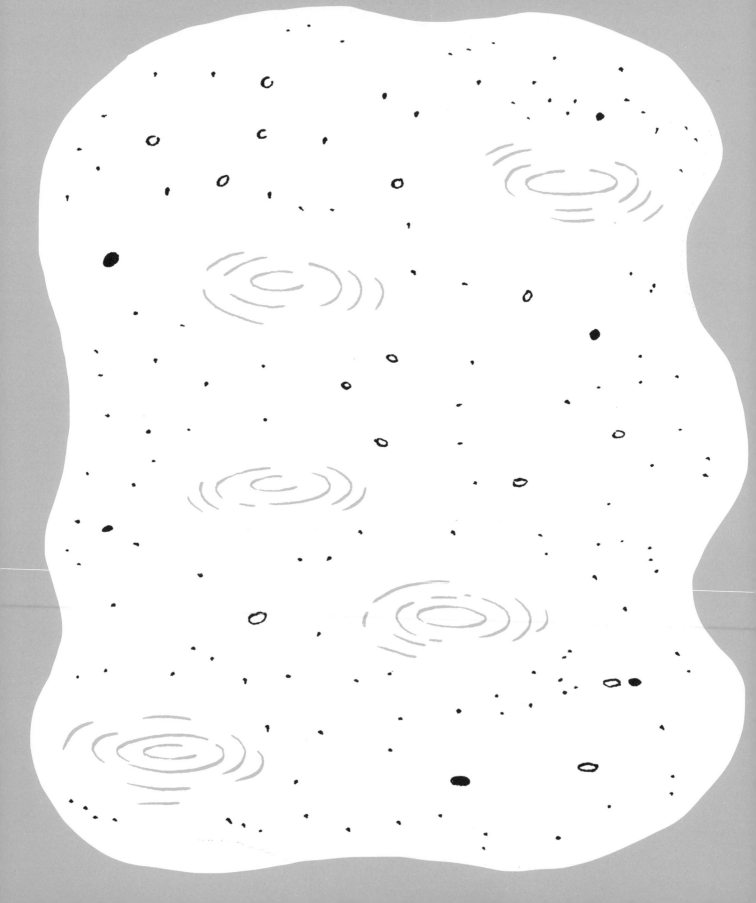

Draw a baby
vampire
learning
how to fly.

Draw the
winner of
this year's
stinky prize.

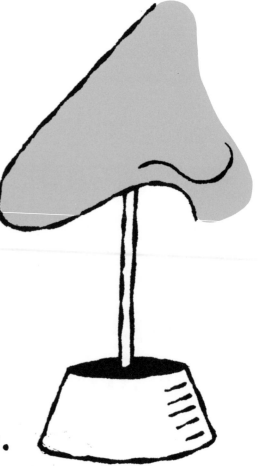

Draw how these bones might fit together.

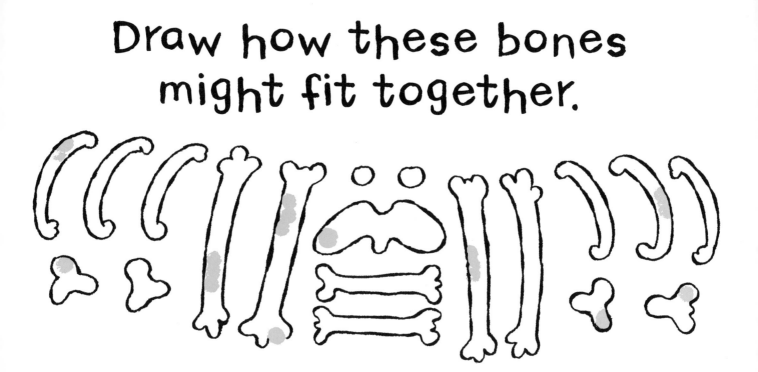

Draw Frankenstein's
monster on a
skateboard.

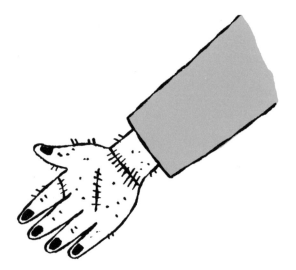

Draw something horrible under this bed.

Draw a giant wobbly sea slug.

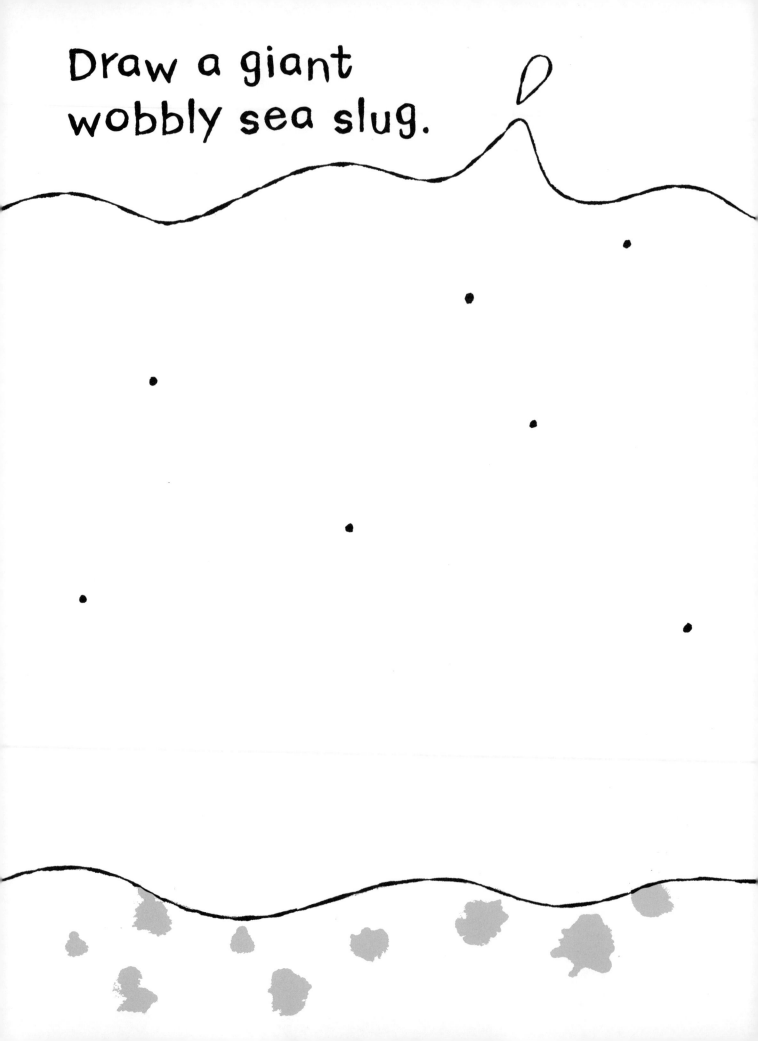

Draw a toy
for this baby
gargoyle.

Draw an anti-vampire kit.

Draw a
slime
cake.

Draw a stench.

Draw a before-and-after poster for the monsters' dental clinic.

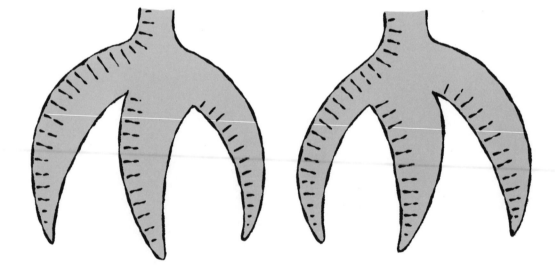

Draw the owner
of these claws.

Draw what's inside this little monster's gift bag.

Draw some
finger
fungus.

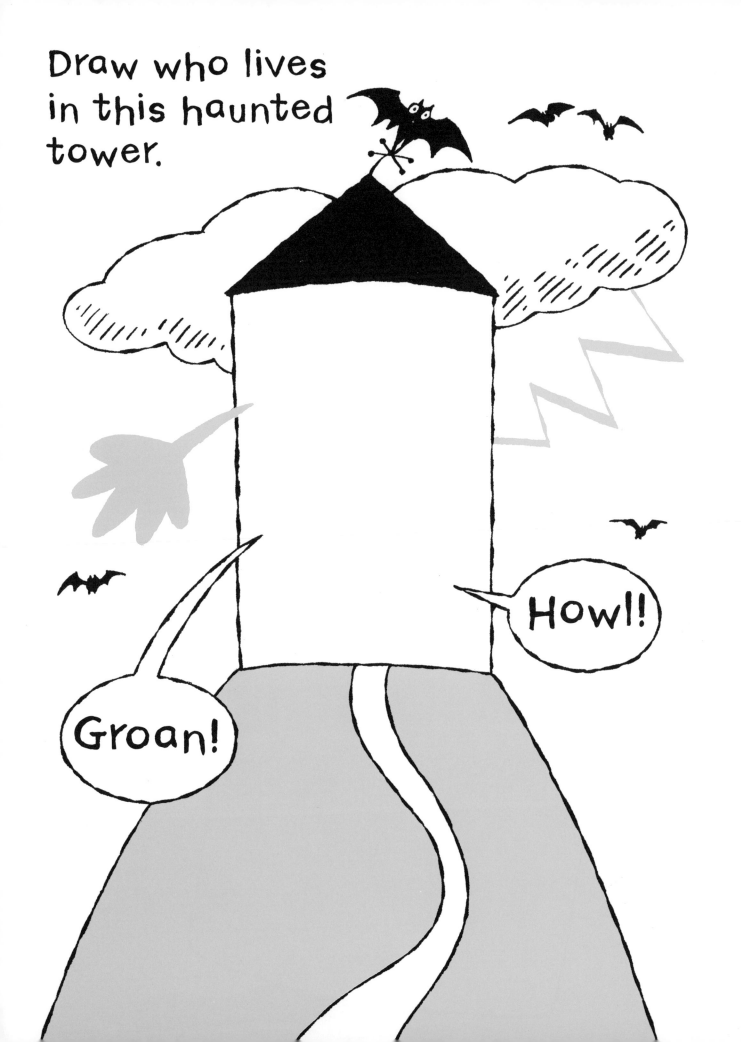

Draw something disgusting in this bottle.

Cold-water
bottle

Draw a monster
with a stomachache.

Draw a housewarming gift for a witch.

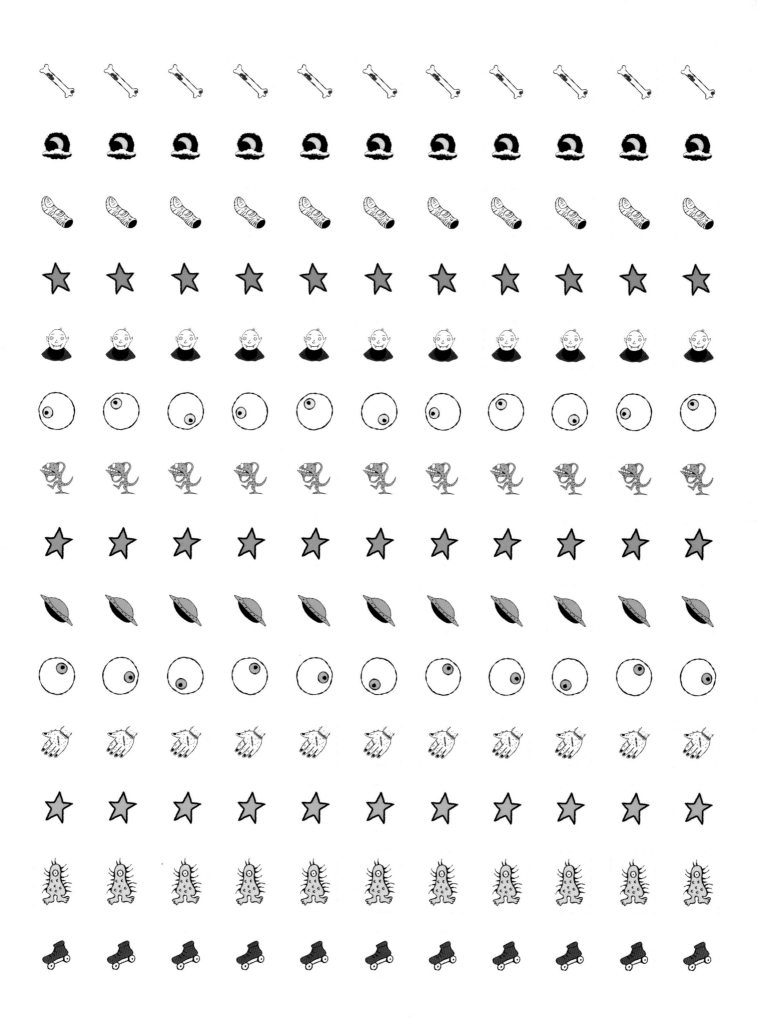

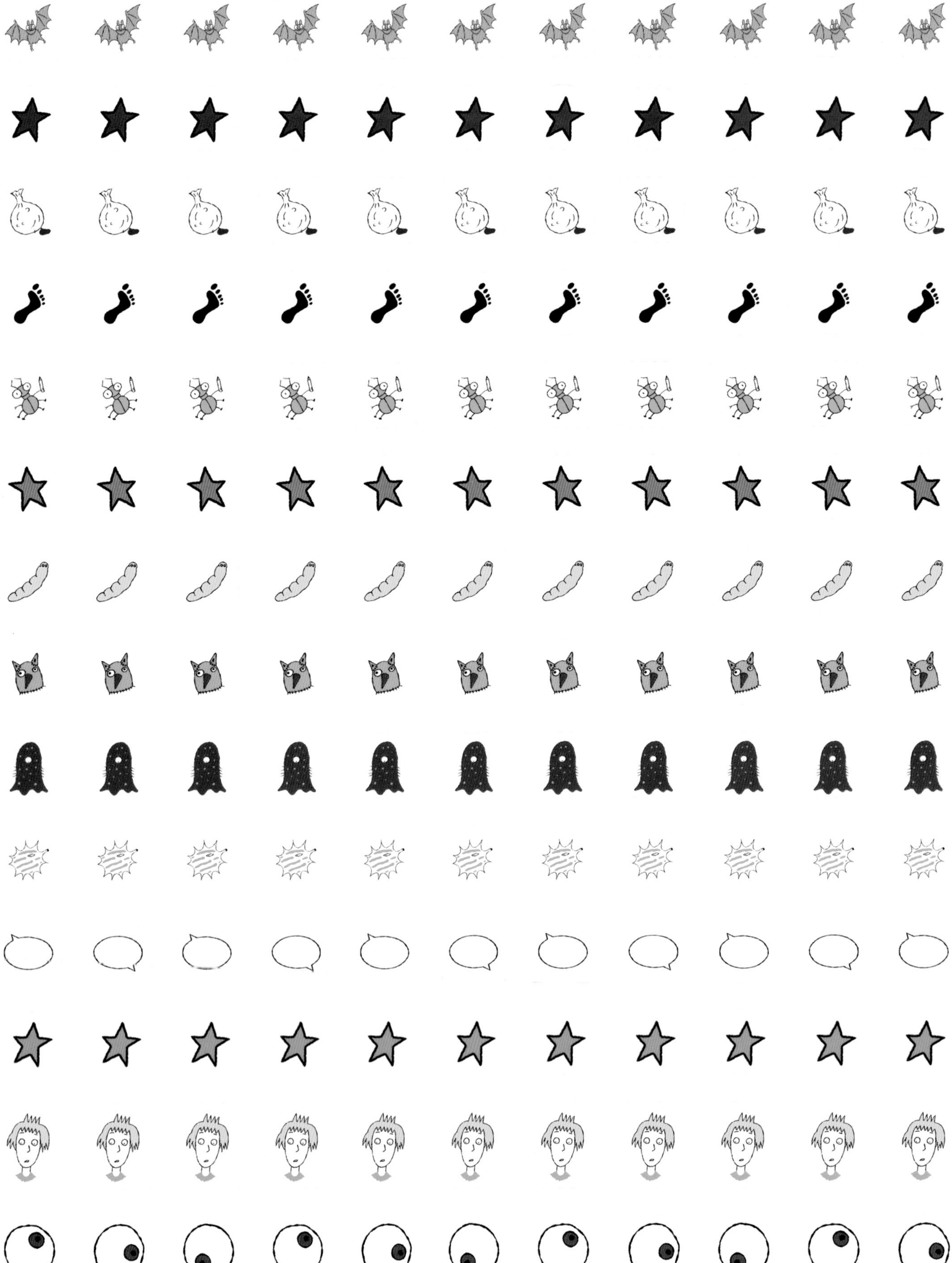

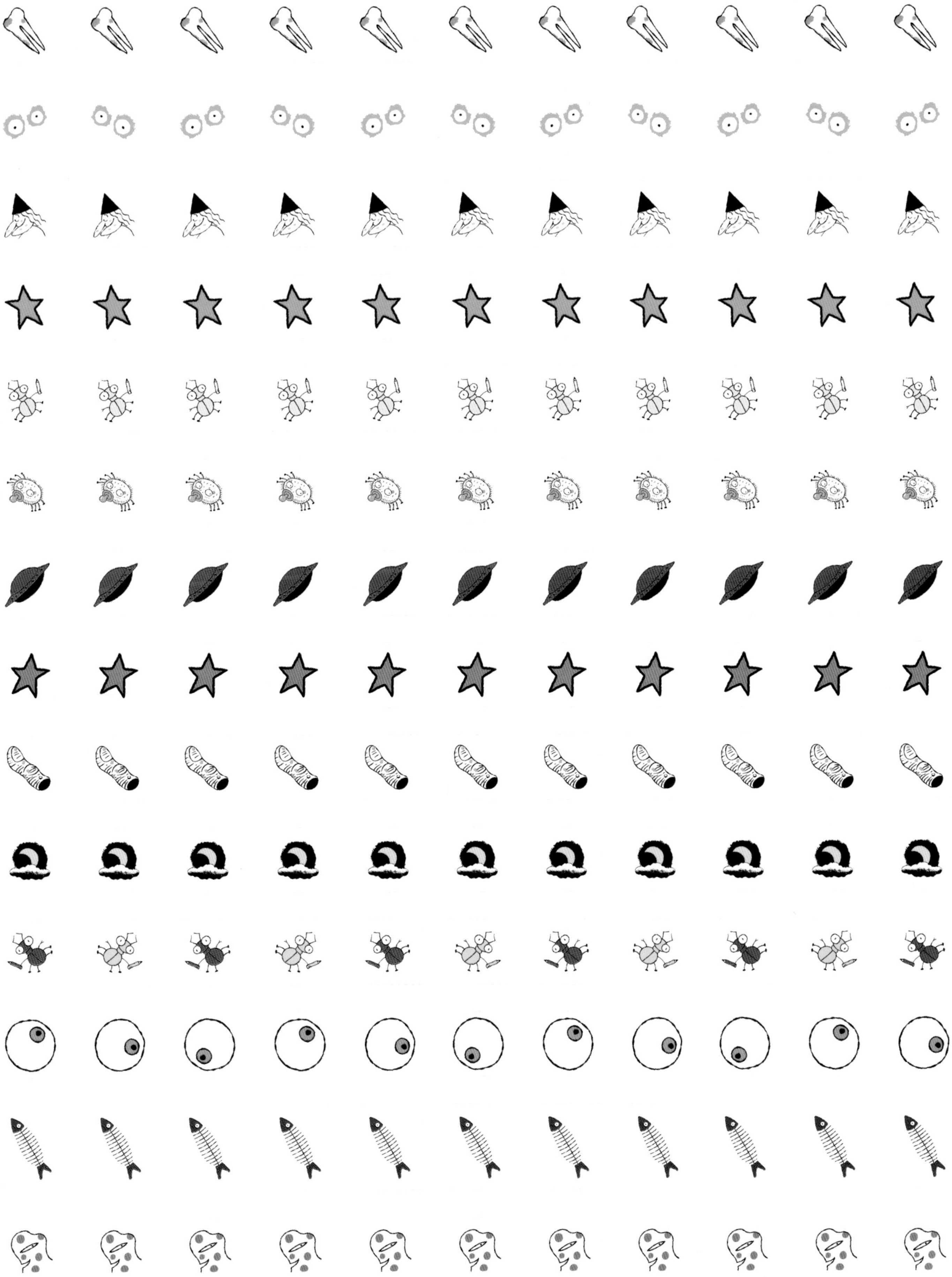

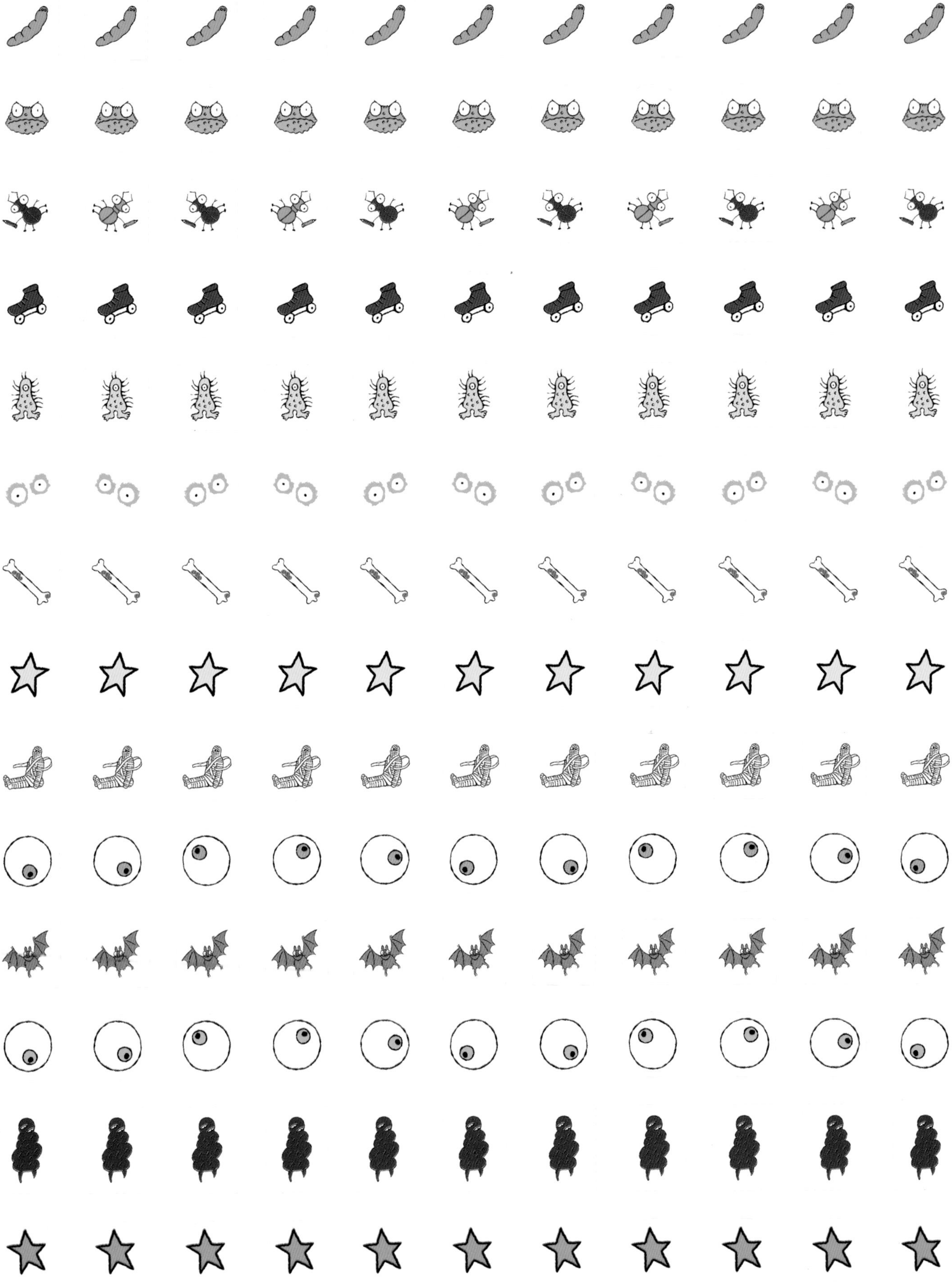

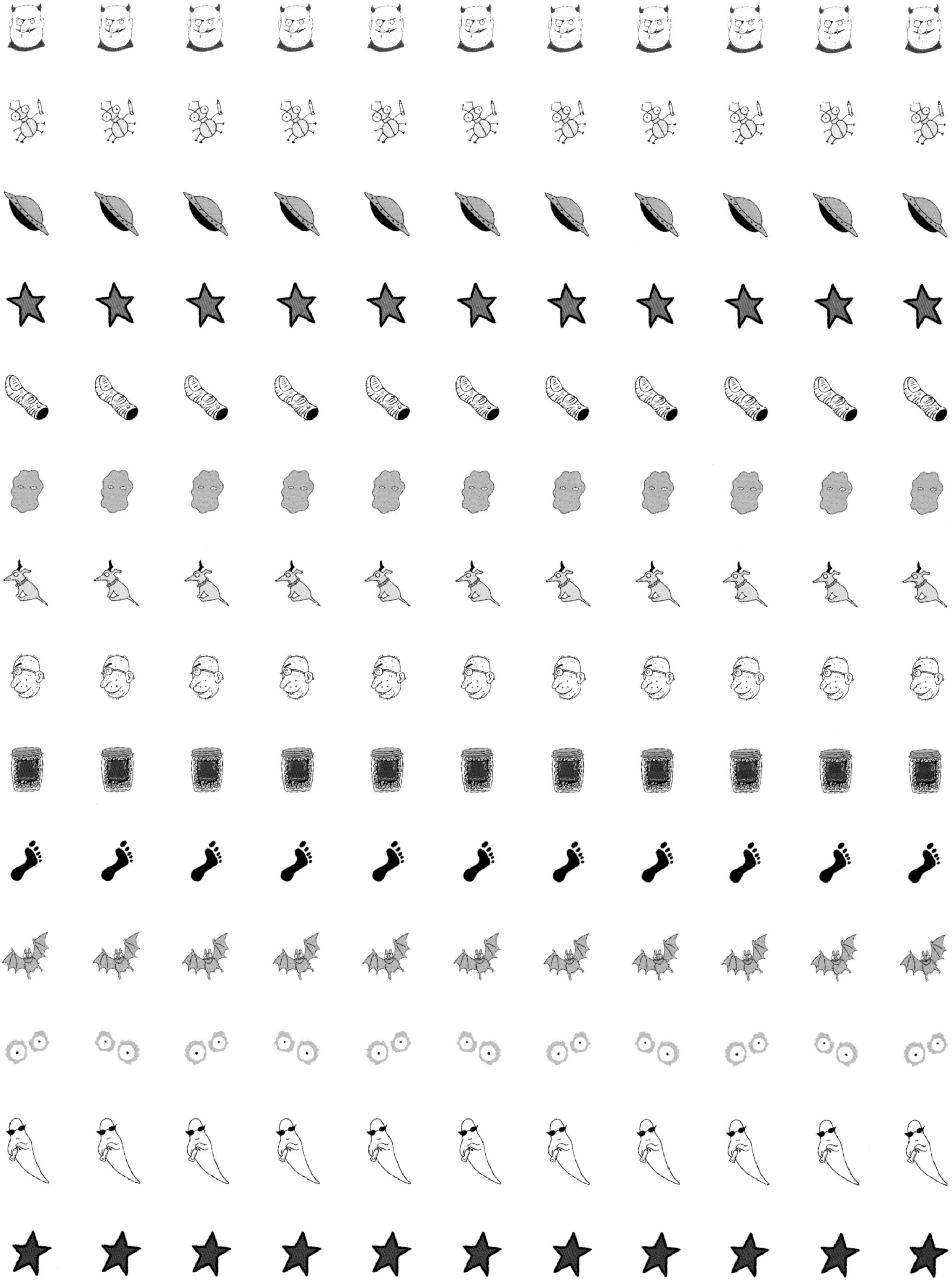

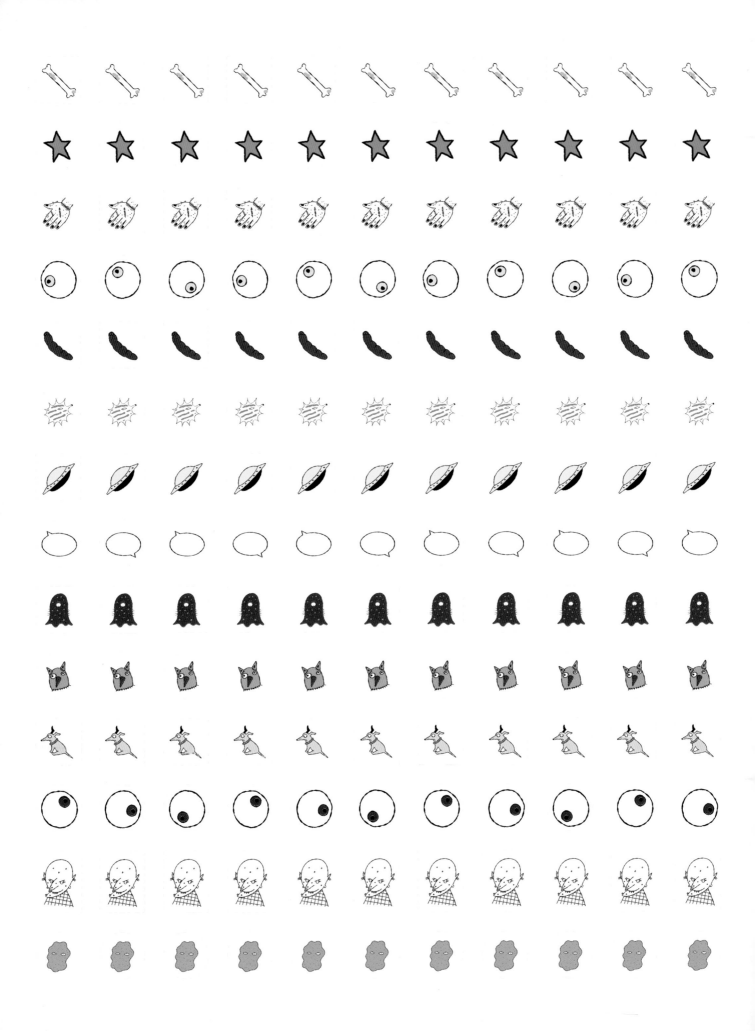